UN STRONG

6 WAYS TO BUILD YOUR
SELF-LOVE MUSCLE:
FRIEND LEAVE YOUR CAPE AT THE DOOR

Teresa Strong Myrick

Acknowledgment

This book was written and produced after the death of my mother Johnnie Mae and six months later, my husband Paul. I received an exuberant amount of love and support from friends, family, and strangers. They supported in every way imaginable. It brought me face-to-face with a couple of trouble spots from my past. One was hearing the word "strong" used to describe how I was handling things. Second was the importance of being vulnerable enough to ask for help getting through that moment. There was a time in my life where I did not think strength and vulnerability could coexist. Because of this, I suffered. I am thankful to everyone who demonstrated, even in the midst of a pandemic, racial injustice and political turmoil, that they could still have the heart to support and love on me. This is for all the strong friends who currently struggle with society's definition and expectations of the word "strong".

It is because of my friends and family I'm able to produce this body of work. I want to specifically acknowledge Trina, Darlene, and Sandra who have been behind the scenes encouraging me and cheering me on. There was a team of beautiful, sweet-spirited young ladies who helped me explore the extent of my outer beauty and who were responsible for my entire book cover: Amber Rose (Make-up Artist), Precious (Love) Igbinosun (Stylist), Clareesse Littles (Photographer), and the wonderful Deanna Hunt (Graphic Designer) who coordinates all things design-related. I made requests from two of my favorite artists, my son Jonathan Griffin (designer of S-T-R-O-N-G) and niece, Nichela Giles (designer of UN) who both came through BIG. Last, but not least, my baby boy Jayson who was the photographer for my first book and has been my little helper from the beginning. He has been a greeter, a server, a deejay, a participant (when no one showed up), and the one who encourages me to dream bigger.

My prayer is that this book gives strong friends the permission to be comfortable in their vulnerability, to ask for help, and to accept the help that is given. Also, to help others to support that one family member or friend who is bench pressing twice his/her weight in responsibility.

Table of Contents

Introduction

First, understand that, UNSTRONG does not equal weak and vulnerable. This book is a journey in building your inner strength. A strength that is reliable – one that does not leave or fail you. A strength that does not depend on the perceptions of others. It does not waiver with the opinions of outside people. This strength is empowering, invigorating, and enlightening. It does not require that you go outside of yourself for validation. You will have it within you — it'll be with you wherever you go. You want that, right? Let's dig in.

Are You the Strong Friend?

1. In charge of everything (strong leadership skills)
2. Highly responsible (or at least seems that way)
3. The one everyone calls on for help
4. Organizer of all family reunions
5. The reasonable one
6. Great giver of advice
7. Unflappable, never seems upset/bothered/overwhelmed
8. Appearing to have everything under control (never needing outside help)
9. Needing a break but afraid that things will fall apart without you.
10. One of many siblings but your parents only call on you.

Do you see yourself in the above? I could continue the list, but I think you get where I am going. Let me be clear, none of the above qualities are bad or wrong. The problem is when you are hurting on the inside from the self-imposed, systematic neglect of self. In other words – on the inside you feel depressed, unfulfilled, unappreciated, resentful, inauthentic, and uninspired.

I feel you, which is why I am writing this book and starting the Un-Strong movement. Friend you can be just as strong on the inside as you portray on the outside. The greatest joy in this is that once you learn and practice self- love, you will feel less pressure to perform. You will feel as if you have more time on your hands and like a weight has lifted off you. Strong friend, it is your right and responsibility to take care of yourself. Inner strength comes from building your self-love muscle.

I was asked, "Is self-love a muscle?". You may be wondering the same thing. Consider the definition of muscle as, "the strength that sustains us". Just as a muscle, your self-love can be built up. As a matter of fact, the more you exercise it, the stronger it (and thereby, you) become. You must feed it with information that builds it, rather than tears it down. Without working on it, it doesn't become strong enough to support a positive, loving state of being. You'll become less capable of fighting off negativity and powerless over the pains and hurts of the past. So, yes, self-love, for the purpose of this book, is a muscle. We will take the time here to build upon what you have and create the type of strength that seeps from the inside out.

I have a bitter-sweet relationship with the word "STRONG". It is actually my maiden name — not just an adjective I threw in to describe myself. It's a name that I've always been incredibly proud of while being an adjective that annoyed me and caused internal conflict.

I first came to dislike the description when my brother died. I was instructed to be strong for my mom. They meant to refrain from crying, don't be too emotional, remain focused, remain dutiful, handle all the affairs, say yes to all the demands on my time and emotions... you get the idea. Sans one moment when I temporarily lost my mind and thought I could bring my brother back to life, I did what was expected of me.

I also lost my apartment, my car, and my drive. I fell out with the church. They are the ones who transferred all their duties onto me and left me unsupported. Did I not matter? I was grieving too! My baby brother, my first best friend, and the only person I'd fight for...had died.

Since I did not allow myself to grieve my brother's death, it hit me hard a year later. I remember being at my mom's and going into his room. All of a sudden, a tsunami of emotions welled up in me as I realized for the first time that he was never coming back. I cried and cried hard. I was fragile after that. Everything bothered me. I could not handle any extra emotion, responsibility, stressor – I would tear up and have to fight back the tears. I called a counselor. I needed help. I had to be strong enough to admit my weakness in the moment. I had to be strong enough to get the necessary assistance to move through this new territory of "feeling."

Strong is overrated and weakness undervalued

It is a part of those catchphrases I love to hate — that go-to adjective when we don't know what else to say. "Be strong; You're strong, you can handle it; You're strong, you'll figure it; You're strong, so you'll be fine." I get it. We want to encourage folks. We don't want them to allow this one moment take to them entirely out.

My concern is that what we perceive as "strong" is the opposite of what it is. This confuses people. Society's definition almost denotes some sort of "Super Power." Undue societal pressure is what it amounts to. It communicates I'm "less than" if I show weakness". Therefore I (we) put on the facade of having it all together and commence the race to perfection. What is seen as a show of weakness is merely, in my opinion, our humanness. We can't be effective humans if we are simultaneously denouncing that which makes us human – feelings, emotions, and the freedom to express them.

Weakness is undervalued. It is undervalued in that
the true meaning of emotional & spiritual strength is
just the opposite of how we have come to see it. There is
strength in showing vulnerability. There is strength in
displaying your emotions without shame or judgment.
Of course, it is also going against the norm, others' expectations,   and what society has dictated to us is to be
strong. This book will talk about my experience and what
it takes to garner strength from our weaknesses. Your
weakness is when you allow yourself to be human and
realize that you cannot (and weren't designed) to do this
life alone. It is in your weakness that you find that you
can get through the hard times. It is where you discover
what you are made of — it is where you learn the lessons
needed for growth. Weakness, I've learned, is the opportunity to grow, build, and strengthen.

When you believe that emotions make you weak and you
are committed to being strong, you will do everything to
not show your feelings. You will do everything to sup-
press these feelings. Emotions are like beach balls that
you're trying to hold up underwater — once you finally
release the ball (emotions), it exits the water with im-
mense force equivalent to the energy needed to keep it
down. The further you push the ball down, the greater
the power created. Emotionally, this is when you, as my
son would say, are going to "go off". You vomit your emotions all over people; you rage violently or break down in
uncontrollable tears.

After the explosion, you will generally feel bad about what you did and/or what you said (or didn't say). You will then commence beating yourself up mentally. You now believe that you are a weakened person because you could not control the emotion's intensity. That you are a person of little worth — that you are "less than". And when you believe this, your actions will follow. You can't go out there and command the world — you can't make your dreams come true in this frame of mind. You cannot get focused and fired up about purpose. You are in a state of believing that you are less of a human, not essential, a failure, not good enough; because you unleashed unresolved, intense, and uncontrolled raw emotion. Do you see how cyclical this is now? You refuse to show feelings when you feel them because you don't want to appear weak; you bury them to show strength. You then explode and feel powerless and vulnerable because of the explosion. However, had you expressed the emotions, at the time you touched them—constructively and healthily — you would be less likely to have the blast of emotions or meltdown. You would have felt the strength that comes with clear, complete, and healthy communication. No feelings left behind.

We do with emotions what we do with past mistakes, past trauma, past disappointments, and poor decisions. We spend a lifetime trying to hide them — not giving them their due respect because of shame and guilt.

The idea here is to **S**top and assess your level of fulfill-
ment, tell the **T**ruth about your past, build your **R**esil-
ience muscle, take **O**wnership of your negative behavior/
attitudes, examine your **N**etwork of support, and get
Going with a strong emotional foundation.

In this book, we are taking a deep dive to examine six
elements that I have discovered that contribute to a
person's inner strength. This formula I found in ret-
rospect as I've looked over my life and the life of those
around me. The themes, although overlooked, are
prevalent in those we deem "strong". I've discovered
through my personal and professional experience what
it means to dig deep and summon that inner strength.
So hang on, because I will undoubtedly shake up some
of the norms in your life and challenge how you are
thinking about strength (yours and others').

Chapter 1 – UN

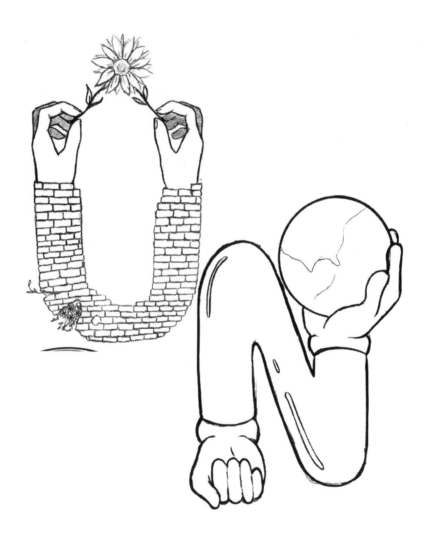

The "UN"

Un-cape. I invite you to take off your cape right here. Leave it at the door of this journey — you won't need it in this space. We are removing the facade of the cape. What you portray as strong is not; it is hiding. It is putting everything before you and in front of you so that you can ignore what's going on within you. The cape is just a cover-up. You put on the mask and commence to rescuing everyone else while neglecting the inner you — the inner child in you who desperately needs an outlet. But no one knows — no one sees, because you're a hero out there in the streets while being a mess behind closed doors. The most damaging part is that you begin to believe what the streets are saying about you and fall in line with their expectations.

When asked if you need anything, what's your response? It's likely, "I'm fine, I'm good, I got it; Oh, It's okay." This only further buries your truth and makes it more challenging to tap into and access. You will not know your true strength until you tap into YOUR truth.

This book is about unmasking — getting to the reality of who you are so you can show up authentically, you can show up with your real, natural strength. You can show up with the strength of your purpose, the strength of who God made and intended you to be, with the power of your uniqueness; your unique talents. What society says it means to be strong, is a fallacy — and it is killing you slowly. And if you don't stop, you will find yourself 50 years old, feeling lost, alone, misunderstood, frustrated, disappointed, full of resent and anger.

Chapter 2 S – Self Assess

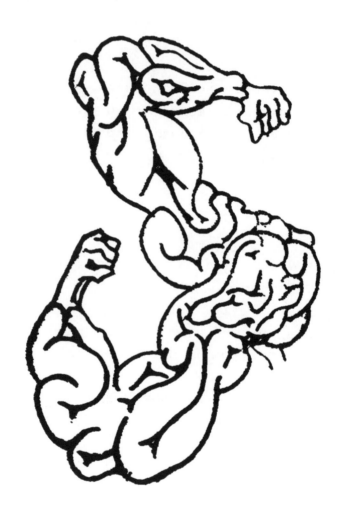

Stop and Self-Assess

Stop and assess where you are right now.
Look at your situation.

Stop and take a breath,

Stop and take a break.

Just stop.

Stop being all the things to all people and nothing to
yourself. Stop filling everybody's plate from the scraps
of yours. You're doing both you and them a disservice.
Stop.

Stop putting conditions on your happiness. Thinking
that you must have this before you can be happy. Choose
happy now, choose joy now. Although happiness can be
fleeting, joy is a state that you can embody deep inside of
you and call upon at any time — even amid all troubles.
Choose not to put a condition on when and how you will
experience joy. I have found myself saying things like,
when I lose 10 pounds I'll be happy, or I have to get this
degree before I am smart enough to go after that dream.
Some may say, I must have children before I can feel like
a woman. Stop putting conditions upon your happiness
and simply decide to choose happiness. Time is precious.
Make the most of your time by choosing joy every day.

Now I know that that's not realistic for everyone. But I also know that there is something that you can be grateful for in your day. I invite you to be more diligent about finding those things to be thankful for. Because that's the thing that will take you out of the funk of life. When you can start to focus on the gratefulness, the good things that happen, and the things you are blessed to have, you can begin to change your energy. You move from a place of victim-hood to a place of power.

Self Assessment

Mirror work. When you look in the mirror. What do you see? Do you see all your flaws, or do you see all the greatness that's within you? For a long time when I looked in the mirror, I did not like what I saw looking back at me. It had nothing to do with how I physically looked. Because even when I was at my best. I did not think I was pretty. I thought I was kind of cute, but I felt I had to have makeup to be attractive. When I looked in the mirror, all I saw were the imperfections in my face. I saw all the acne and acne scars. I saw nothing else. And it's only when I look back — as I've gotten older and look back at those pictures — that I see how beautiful I was. I did not see myself as a person. I did not look into my eyes and say, "I love you, I love the person that you are", because I didn't. I felt so much shame that I was afraid to even face anything close to knowing who I was. To me, I was only that abused little girl who was taken advantage of; who was made to feel like crap. The girl whose voice wasn't necessary, whose thoughts didn't matter. So check your mirror. What do you see reflected back at you? You may not be able to see the beauty that others see in you. Instead, you see the flaws that you believe and that have been compounded by other people's judgment. So when people say something negative to you — and it brings you down — it's likely because you have some buy-in. It mirrors what you already are saying about yourself. So, therefore, you allow yourself to go down that road of self-abuse.

Why can't we do the same thing when people say something positive about us — when someone says, "Oh, you're so pretty"; when someone says, "Oh, you're so intelligent." Those of us who have had some traumas haven't learned to love ourselves. We reject compliments, we minimize our accomplishments; we think people are lying to us when they say those things. So check your mirror. What do you see? What stories are you believing?

Stop punishing yourself for being different. After I stopped and reflected and realized that I am an introvert, I learned about myself, I learned that although I like to be out and have fun and party and laugh out loud, I am also thrilled to be at home with a book and my journal. I had to stop comparing myself to what other people thought was acceptable. I had to stop comparing my fun to other people's enjoyment. Don't judge yourself for what brings you joy; your happiness might be getting seven hours of sleep. Let it be. Maybe you no longer want to hang out all night because it doesn't make you feel good. I remember when I was in my 20's, I loved to go clubbing.

I also remember the moment that it changed for me. I recognized it in the moment. I remember feeling over-dressed, disgusted with the atmosphere, mad because no one was dancing, and judging people for being drunk. I knew at that point that clubbing wasn't for me any-more. From that point on, I declined the invitations and explored other options that allowed me to dance and enjoy good music. The point is to honor your needs, your desires, your wants, and be okay with it. Don't com-pare yourself to other people; your experience has to be unique because you are unique. You are made like no one else. You may change and evolve at a different rate than those currently around you, and that is okay.

Chapter 3 T-
Truth & Transparency

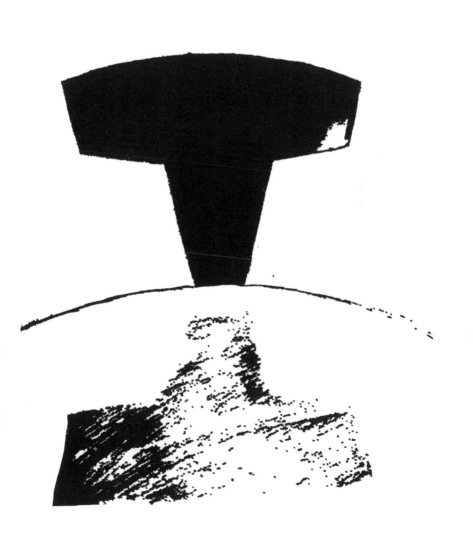

Truth & Transparency

Who are you? Be truthful to yourself. Get to know yourself—no shame or blame. You are not the things that happened to you. You must look at your past differently. What good can you glean from it? Focus on your resilience. Know that you've made it through every hard time that you have encountered thus far.

We have a choice. We can focus on all the negative and live in that, or we can go back, gather the positive aspects of our lives, and change our internal narrative. Stop giving the negativity of your life more power than blessings. It is difficult to see your greatness when you are looking through a negative lens. To allow the negative of your past to define you is self-defeating. It does not give credence to your effort and ability to get through it. Go on a search. Go back and name the blessings over your life. Look at the difficult times to examine how and why it was needed in your life. I believe that nothing happens that God did not allow and that all things are happening for our good. Not an easy assignment AND a much needed one.

Be true to you about your habits, coping mechanism, your good traits, and your not so good traits. Be true to you about you. Recognize those things around you that bring you joy as well as those that are upsetting your peace. Stop tolerating messiness in your life (figuratively and literally). It is time to get honest and get clear. Acknowledge the conversations that are needed that are not being had. You undoubtedly, in all your STRONG FRIEND identity, have some things that you are scared to address. What are they? Take the power away from that fear by naming it. Where is it that you REALLY need to stand up for yourself? When do you need to start saying NO? And when do you need to say HELL YES?

Boundaries are necessary to maintain your peace. Your peace is your responsibility. Boundaries are crucial in cultivating and maintaining your renewed truth. Establish them and retain them. The illustration I like to give is one involving my grandbabies: I have six grands. At the time of this writing, they were all under the age of ten. The range is from three to 10. We, at one time, lived in a house with a fenced backyard and they loved to play back there. I never worried about them getting outside of the confines of that fence. The boundaries were clear. They had an established structure. There was no fudging where they were and where they should be. Its foundation was sturdy and there were no parts where there were holes or breaks.

This is how I would encourage you to set your boundaries. Initially, make them rigid so that you recognize when they are being challenged. You will know when you are relaxing them; it will be clear.

We later moved to a place where there was a huge back-yard – no fence. My grandbabies could go out in the backyard and see four yards of open space. Although there were other houses, it looked, to them, like wide-open space. This presented as a bit of a challenge. Now for the older ones, I could say, hey, be careful of where you are, watch where the end of the house is, and stop there. The boundary was there but not as present as a fence. It was a whole gray area in terms of where they were to stop . They got it, so they would be mindful of it. They would go over it by a bit, catch themselves and come back. Now the little ones had no idea and did not care. At one point, we looked up, and the younger ones were four yards over, playing and having a good time as if nothing was wrong because they did not recognize or respect that invisible boundary.

You will have people in your life who will challenge your boundaries. Some by a little and others by a lot. For some, it will be inadvertent. For others, it will be in-tentional to test if you mean it. The latter will have the audacity to be mad at you for setting and keeping bound-aries . Understand that their response is not about you; it's about them. You are undoubtedly disrupting the way they do business and upsetting THEIR norms.

I'm telling you that people will not recognize, respect, or give any thought to your invisible (unspoken) boundar-ies. They will go as far as you will allow them; it's up to you to establish AND maintain them. You can't get mad at people for crossing boundaries that you did not set.

Just like you must tend to a fence to maintain its integrity, so must you treat your personal boundaries.

If you want to maintain your sanity level and peace while building your inner strength, you must examine those areas of your life where you are feeling the least satisfaction. What are you allowing in your life that is no longer giving you good results? What are you doing just to "keep the peace"? What are you doing to make others happy? Where are you saying yes when you want to say no?

Ask for what you want.

To be strong and exhibit strength in the real sense of the word, mentally and emotionally, you must learn and permit yourself to ask for what you want. Stop settling for "less than". In the same tone of showing up authentically, you must be acutely aware of what it is that you want. It is imperative to break away from other people's expectations of you. You must determine what is true for you.

I grew up a good girl, trying to be perfect to not cause my mom any undue stress. I was the oldest. My mom had lost my dad to murder. Then there was domestic violence with my brother's father. (I wrote about this in detail in my first book, "Attacked In Anger, Died In Love") I never rebelled, got into trouble, or talked back – none of that. I also suppressed everything. I didn't cry, didn't show anger, and wouldn't even laugh out loud. This created a pattern of me doing what I thought was acceptable to blend in and not be noticed. I had no clue who I was. I had no personality of my own. I tried on other people's characteristics to see if it felt right. Can you relate? In my 40's, after deciding to work on me "no matter what," I finally discovered, honored, and permitted myself to have favorite things. I also found my voice and gained the inner strength to express it fully through public speaking, writing, and life coaching.

You may find that you are doing the same. You are doing what your friends, kids, spouse, and parents enjoy doing to "keep the peace." You may also be suppressing the things that you desire for fear of judgment – yours and theirs.

Quite frankly, you probably don't think yourself worthy enough to put your desires & needs on the table. However, when you take inventory of how you're feeling; how content you are with your life, you will find that very likely you're not. To live in this life with discontent is a disservice to you and everyone else around you. Find a way to incorporate the things that you like doing into your life. It may require compromise and a bit of discomfort at first. However, in the present you are making compromises every day. Every day that you don't tap into who you are, you compromise your self-worth and value. So, is that worth it? Because the compound effect of that, I believe, is depression. But then, you look STRONG to everyone else, right? You appear happy. You appear content. You are lying to yourself and them.

> **Facebook post from Feb 15, 2021**
> "I struggle sometimes with asking for exactly what I want
> I will change my request to what's reasonable.
> I won't want to seem like I'm being extra.
> I don't want to inconvenience others with my "lil desires"
> Sometimes I don't feel worthy of the request
> At times, I'm afraid of what the response "might be"
> Well today and from now on, I give myself permission
> to ask for EXACTLY what I want and let the chips fall
> where they may.
> I can no longer be disappointed when I don't get what I
> didn't ask for. (read that again)
> Is this your struggle as well?"

The biblical truth of who you are is that you are beautifully, wonderfully, and uniquely made. You are not meant to blend in.

Check your commitments – what are you more committed to: the truth of who you are or the misery in forgoing your purpose to appease others?

Chapter 4 R – Resiliency

Resilience

"...you turned my wailing into dancing; you removed my sackcloth and clothed me with joy, that my heart may sing your praises and not be silent. LORD my God, I will praise you forever." ~ Psalm 30:11-12

Resilience is the ability to keep getting back up. Keep living until you die. See yourself conquering your goals. Don't take failures personally—no only means to go about it differently.

Resilience cannot exist without failure. Fear of failure stunts your growth. Every time you fall, you should commit to getting back up with a new lesson.

Resiliency builds the character needed to succeed. That would mean that failures are essentially growth opportunities.

If you are not failing, you are probably not in action due to fear.

Action is the antidote to fear.

I have never believed that I can't get through something or that I can't survive without someone. I see people posting about how they'll, "never be the same or never be okay" after a death, divorce, or job loss. I came to realize that I'm built differently. I credit this to my mom, who I believe is the origin of this belief in how she kept going. She had evolved so much and gone through so much by the time she was diagnosed with cancer that she couldn't fathom not getting through it. She lived until she died. She was winning until the game was over, and she realized her opponent won by a hair. I get that now because I am feeling the same way. There were expectations of how I should act, how I should feel, and what I should do after losing both my mom and my husband within six months of one another. There was judgment around my action. Being strong and resilient is to realize that you are a unique individual. You will permit yourself to go about life to support yourself and honor your purpose. You will not worry about conforming to the "shoulds" of the world.

Because of the work I've done, mentally, emotionally, and spiritually to heal, I can show up authentically in my grief. It doesn't mean that I am sad every day because I'm not happy every day either. But I don't feel like I won't get through it. I feel like I will, I feel like I am — so I continue to behave and act in accordance. We don't know how to stop. We don't know how to give up. And when I say, "we", I'm talking about Johnnie Mae (my mom) and me. It's not something that's in our DNA. I didn't see it in my grandma either who just kept going. We do, however, know how to take breaks, pray, recoup, have fun, laugh out loud, dance like no one was watching, and bring joy & light into every room.

Take inventory. You are resilient. You've made it through
every obstacle that you've come across. You survived.
You made it. You are still here. Every day you have
another opportunity to try again. Enjoy the ride, learn
the lessons, try multiple times. There is no limit to how
many times you can try; just be sure to incorporate
something different every time. When you've taken yourself as far as you can take yourself, be unstrong enough
to ask for help.

Chapter 5 O – Own your ish

"Let us test and examine our ways, Let us turn back to the Lord" ~Lamentations 3:40

O is for Ownership

— taking responsibility for where you are right now. Take moral inventory of yourself. You have made decisions that have hurt you and others. Admit it, make amends. Ask for forgiveness. Forgive yourself. Own your mess. Own your strengths and your weaknesses. Own your past failures. Own your laziness, procrastination, and fears. Own the fact that you have the freedom to choose. You are where you are based on YOUR previous DECISIONS. Own the lessons you've learned. What's your part of the "bad" marriage, poor sibling relationships, unemployment, where you live, what you drive, your career, etc. But don't stay there. Looking backward while walking forward will cause you to fall.

When you are overly committed to your past, you impede your progress.

Be willing to extract the lesson. Some of your negative behavior and bad habits stem from unresolved childhood issues – own it. Be ready to get the help needed to release the emotions that are driving the action.

Triggers. Own your triggers. Your triggers belong to you. They live inside of you. However, if you give the power of being triggered to people, places, and things, you have given up control over your life. You are forever a victim. Understand that you are allowing your emotions to be triggered by something immovable and unchangeable. Therefore, putting your energy into changing other people, places, and things is a waste of your time and energy. It is beyond your realm of control. The power that the good Lord has given you is the power to choose. You can decide to change the way you respond to those triggers. You can learn to understand why those things cause you to feel overly emotional when you see or hear them. What past event is it triggering? What within you is being bothered or shifted by something outside of you? Examining these questions would be a better use of your energy.

There are three things that you cannot change. You cannot change other people, your past, nor God's will for your life. To try would be futile and contribute to your eventual insanity.

Now, when I say you can't change your past, I also know that your history comes up in your life, and that's why the trigger is the trigger. The outside thing is triggering a past hurt. It is causing you an emotional response to an external stimulus. That's where you must start your work. Here is where you exercise the strength of who you are and tap into the inner you; the person who survived and overcame. Here is where you stop allowing others to control you and use your triggers against you. Can you imagine the strength you'll exhibit and feel when you don't respond as expected? Whew, chile!

Chapter 6 N- Network

Network

There is strength in numbers and you, my friend, need a team. A team that sees you for who you are becoming. They do not hold you hostage; to your past nor to your limitations.

Be open to attracting like-minded individuals with diverse talents. A person who is a visionary and sees the big picture, a person who motivates you and sees you beyond your limitations, a practical one who will keep you grounded, and an action-driven friend who will guide you to take the next step. Your crew should be moving in a way that stretches you beyond your norm.

You are only as strong as your support system. Don't take this for granted. Don't get so self-sufficient that you become self-destructive. Part of conforming to the world's definition of what it is to be "strong" is looking and acting as if we have everything under control and don't need anyone for anything. This manner of thinking makes you both your strongest AND weakest link. How is that working for you?

I am currently operating in a new reality as I've recently become a widow. I realize that I am low-key worried about something breaking that my husband would usually fix. What if the a/c goes out again, the washing machine stops working, my car breaks down, the sink clogs up, etc.? I found relief knowing that we have built relationships over the years, that I can now draw upon for support. However, what this requires of me is to ask for help where I didn't have to before. I admitted to the fact that I do not have this completely under control on my own. I cannot rely on my abilities at this moment. To maintain my peace, I had to be open to the "giftings" of others.

Now, it is also true that I could Google the remedies and attempt to handle all of these things myself. I can tell you that I would've been stressed out, depressed, and anxious. Also, I deny others the opportunity to be a blessing when I refuse their help. Believe it or not, there are still good people in the world who genuinely like to help others and who are gifted in doing so.

This next concept may be hard to grasp for many of us strong folk: if you have the means to hire, hire. Strong friend, hire a housekeeper. Hire a cook. Get a nanny. Is this causing you some resistance? Did you just say, "I would never!"? " How about, "Oh, WE don't do that"?

As someone once told me, when I had the same reaction, MY gifts are in other places. Some people love to cook, clean, and take care of children and are looking for employment. Bless them by giving them work AND by allowing them to work in their giftings. I needed to hear that. I was becoming stressed out by my house's condition – it was cluttered, the boys didn't clean well enough for me, and I didn't have time. The most blaring resistance I felt was the childhood pattern of beliefs that had me feeling "less than" because my house wasn't clean. But to HIRE someone?! Unheard of. You are not a good wife, mother, woman, man, husband, father... if you can't keep your home in order. Better yet, YOU ARE LAZY. Sound familiar?

Why are we applying that antiquated concept to today's reality of what it is to be a fully functioning family? Remember, design your life in a way that supports YOUR purpose. Let's examine. Where could you use additional help? Who could you reach out to? How much can you afford to reallocate? What could you focus more on if you had support?

Chapter 7 G – Go/Goal Setting

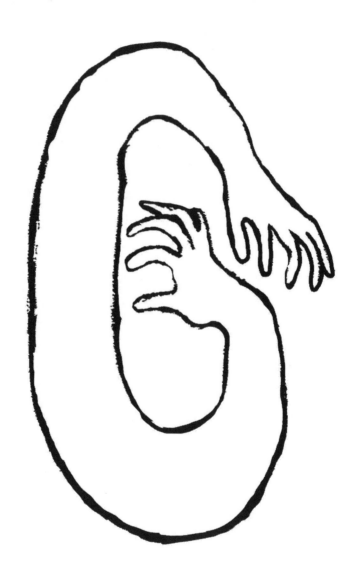

Go

Get into action. Get going. Go do and be. Don't just talk about it, be about it. "Don't die with your dreams inside of you." – Les Brown

You build your strength while in action. Do what you said you would do. The more you keep your promises to yourself, the better you feel about yourself. When we make plans and repeatedly fail to get into action, we begin to devalue our words. There is a tremendous amount of strength in being a person of your word.

Action is the anecdote to failure, procrastination, fear, and stagnation. And get this, it does not have to be perfect action. Perfection is an illusion. It is an excuse and a mask for fear. Your activity can be baby steps or massive movement – it all counts. If you don't go, you'll never know. And maybe that is okay with you. My guess is that if you are reading this book, it is not. But for the sake of argument, think of all the people who won't get helped if you don't do that thing that God has given you to do. You have a book that needs to be written, a conversation that needs to be had, a story that needs to be told, a business to start, a nonprofit to build. Someone is waiting for your account of triumph to give them hope. How many times have you heard or read a story of someone who overcame the odds to do something they've always dreamed of doing? Did it inspire you? Did it encourage you to make changes? Did it bring you out of a dark place, knowing that someone else survived hard times?

You are that for someone else. Don't keep them waiting. They are dying to hear from you. As my mom would always say, "Tomorrow is not promised to you, do what you need to do today." Wearing the mask of STRONG has kept the real you hidden for way too long. Tell me, how much longer do you want to suffer behind the mask and under the heaviness of that cape? They are suffocating you.

If you are ready, let's get to work by reflecting on the beginning of this book – your level of satisfaction with your life. On a scale of 1 to 10, with ten being completely satisfied, how would you rate your level of joy? What does it cost you to stay at that level? What would it take to level-up by one? What would your life look like once you level-up? What belief is keeping you where you are?

Conclusion

The Choice is Yours

The last part of this book is about the choice to heal. Why is healing necessary? It speaks to the inner strength. It addresses your outward behaviors, habits, fears, and responses from the inside out. It has the power to change the trajectory of your legacy. Recovery changes your experience of the world around you. It also changes how the world experiences you. You teach others how to treat you. Healing teaches YOU how to treat and respect yourself. When you choose YOU, you become more attractive to others. Taking on the strong friend persona is in some cases a trauma response. It keeps all the attention off you and onto others. It keeps you from being truly seen. It protects you from dealing with your own stuff. You get to pretend that you don't hurt, you don't care, and are unbothered. You wear it as a badge of honor while secretly feeling as if no one would care anyway. I speak from experience.

How to heal when others around you are not ready. Know that your choice to heal will challenge the normalcy of those around you. It doesn't necessarily mean they don't support you; they don't know the result. Most people are afraid of change and committed to complacency. Your job is to be aware of this and know that everyone won't choose to heal. And if they do, it may not be at the same pace or level as you. Also, recognize that we all have a story, and you may not be fully aware of the depth of another person's inner struggles. Give them grace while you continue your work. Invite them on the journey, but don't become discouraged when they don't accept. Become a living example of living a life dedicated to healing and revealing your best version of yourself. I have to warn you here that some may distance themselves from you. That's okay too. It is expected. As you heal, your habits will change. You may not want to hang out, drink, club, smoke, overeat, shop, fight, work at a thankless job, listen to negativity, gossip....you get where I'm going. Don't worry; you will begin to attract those who will support your healing. Give yourself grace and continue to do your work.

Honoring your process. Know that there are layers to this. Thirty years of shame, blame, self-abuse, playing small, and suppressing emotions will not disappear in an instant (usually). You will continuously be evolving. Your past will show up in odd places and odd times. Remain committed to the process. When something comes up for you a trigger, take the time to self-reflect and self-assess. What's the truth about what happened (what are the facts, absent the emotions). Think about this: you added feeling to the words you heard or the action you witnessed. Own that it is something within YOU that needs to be addressed. Remember that you are resilient and able to figure it out and get through the moment.

There is healing in forgiveness.

Forgiveness of self and others. Heal to forgive – yourself and others. First of all, let's be honest. We have done some things that we are not proud of. We could probably write a list of sins that we could ask forgiveness for. Some little lies told, gossip spoken, hurtful words said in anger, disappointments, promises broken....to name a few. And let's be honest, you could, for the most part, live your life without ever hearing anyone say, "I forgive you." Out of sight, out of mind, right?

That is precisely how the person who wronged you is feeling. On the other hand, you are trying to hold them accountable for your pain and make them feel the pain you feel. You are exerting all of the energy while they are moving on with their life. Your forgiving them does not absolve them of wrongdoing; it sets you free. You acknowledge that there is a power greater than you who can and will handle their misconduct. It is having faith that all things are working for your good. Chasing them down or harboring ill feelings within you affects only you. Permit yourself to forgive. Be willing to forgive and pray for the release of forgiveness. Then forgive yourself in the same manner for all the things you "should have done," all the things "you knew better than" to do, your mistakes, and your bad decisions. Today is a new day with new opportunities. Embrace you're now. Be present with who you are and who you are becoming.

Healing is a choice and is available to all of us. We must be willing to do the work and be uncomfortable. You can either embrace the discomfort of breakthroughs or stay committed to the comforts of your misery.

My journey. Over time, I've always disliked those overly simple, solution statements telling me what I should do:

Just forget about it.

Get over it.

Get your breakthrough.

It's mind over matter

Brush it off

You'll be alright

Just don't think about it

Those statements never gave me relief or real direction. It felt, instead, that they were minimizing the seriousness of my situation. Then there was the high-level, intellectual advice that did not change the emotions that I was carrying. In my experience, this advice told me "the how" and "the what" (which were helpful) but did not address the why (the driver) of my bad habits, poor decisions, inability to get in action, and feelings of unworthiness. The emotions were buried in my belly — in my chest and I could not get relief from them. That's why neuro transformational results coaching was so attractive to me. After I learned of it, witnessed it, and experienced it, I was hooked. It was the thing that took me over the edge.

Life Recovery principles permitted me to need healing. Life recovery said, okay, you don't have to hide it anymore. I didn't have to be embarrassed by my past anymore. I could recognize that even though I "got saved" (became a Christian), the residual results of what happened in my past could still bother me. The Life Recovery Process allowed me to understand that I did not need to be perfect to be loved by God. I refer to both these modalities when I coach my clients. You must seek and find the formula that works for you. Don't give up when one counselor doesn't work out, or one method doesn't give you the breakthrough or transformation you expected. You must commit for the long haul. This is your LIFE, for heaven's sake.

I want to give you your permission to heal. You don't need MY permission, but sometimes it helps to hear it. Know that healing is a choice. Recovery is your right, and it is available to you. Healing is not passive; it is active. We must be willing to dig deep and touch some of that hurt so that we can move through it. You cannot heal what you are unwilling to confront. We spend many years suppressing those feelings because we don't know what to do with them. My invitation to you is to do something to start that process. Find someone you trust who also can deal with you in that space. It must be someone who can guide you to and through the pain – not someone who will leave you in it. That's important.

When life Knocks the When out of you

My grandma had a saying, "Stop fittin' and fartin' around". Translation? Stop playing around with my time — stop procrastinating. My grandma never learned to drive. She depended on other people to take her where she needed to go. Whenever she would find herself waiting around for someone to come and get her, she would say, "they just be fittin' and fartin' around. They need to come on over here and take me where I need to go'. One of my mom's favorite sayings was, "Tomorrow is not promised" or "Time is not on your side." If it's something you want to do, get it done today if you are able.

Towards the end of my mom's life, I was so concerned about her becoming overly tired or overextending herself. I would say, well, when you feel better, we'll do this; when you have a little bit more energy, we'll do that. She would look at me and say, I'm always going to be tired. The doctor said I'm just going to be tired; there's no getting around it, so I might as well just do it. And still, there are a lot of things that I didn't ask her to do or introduced to her because I was waiting until she felt better. I was waiting till she had more energy. I was waiting for her to look as if she had the stamina to do whatever it was and not be so exhausted once we finish. But she didn't have that thought. She kept going until she could not. So I kept wandering, and I kept expecting the "When" to come. And she kept doing life. Life took the "when" away from me.

When she feels better, then we will take this trip that she's always wanted to take. I said that when she feels better, I'll set up that in-home massage that she's always wanted but never had. When she's feeling better and can dance the way she wants to dance, I will throw her a massive party for her birthday. "When" did not come. The lesson in all of this is in of the one of the last things she uttered to me before she took her last breath, "Live your life, Tee". What I heard in that simple statement was: live your life without waiting for perfect conditions, without worrying about the opinions of others, without the re-strictions/limitations of my past. What I also heard was, you know your purpose now, so go live it.

The greatest lesson of her illness and her battle with cancer was that she lived until she died; she would not allow anyone to treat her like she was sick. You couldn't treat her like she was dying, and you had to treat her as she was — a living human being. Because, as she said, "I may have cancer, but you can go out there and get hit by a car and die today. I just know what I'm most likely to die of. We're all getting closer to death every day." She didn't want any pity.

The purpose of this writing is to encourage you to live YOUR life. Don't fall prey to other people's expectation of you. Don't continue to relive your past. You are not your failures, bad decisions, and certainly not what others did to you. Don't fall prey to what the people are saying or may say about you. God is ultimately in control.

Some people stopped living long before their bodies die. They stopped living and started to wait on death. They live miserable, unfulfilled lives. But for those who will take control of their lives and orchestrate a life of happiness and joy, they actively live until their body gives out. The one thing I've seen with life and death over my years is that sometimes the human spirit will outlive the body. Other times, the body outlives the human spirit. How will you choose?

I invite you to choose to live an abundant, unapologetic, un-strong life.

About the author

Teresa is a former police officer, victim advocate, and child & family counselor which exposed her to people at many phases of inner hurt. She is also a homicide survivor (her father was murdered when she was a child), a child who grew up in domestic violence, and a survivor of child sexual molestation.

The combination of personal and professional experience fuels her passion to help others break free from past hurts and create the life they deserve. She knows how unresolved past hurt leads to the hurting of others, self-abuse, and/or allowing oneself to be hurt.

She now serves others as a *Certified Neuro-Transformational Results Coach*, speaker, and Best-Selling Author. She shares the principles, practices, and techniques that were used to help her, to now help others. Those who have attended Teresa's transformational workshops, participated in her *BreakFree 360* private coaching, or have heard Teresa speak, have left with more confidence, a clear purpose, and have been inspired to follow dreams that are true to who they are.

Website: http://mytstrongnetwork.com
Instagram.com/teestrongspeaks
Facebook.com/teestrongspeaks